T0026515

Which Job Is Right for You?

VISTA®
HIGHER LEARNING

Boston, Massachusetts

ELA

A community is the group of people who live or work in a certain area.

There are many different types of jobs. There are jobs where you work alone. There are jobs where you work as a team. There are jobs where you work inside. There are jobs where you work outside. There are jobs in communities, cities, offices, stores, hospitals, and restaurants.

What are different jobs like? What are the **advantages**? What are the **disadvantages**? Which job is right for you?

mail truck

letter

packages

Mail carriers work for the post office. They bring people letters and packages. Some mail carriers drive mail trucks and others walk. They carry mail from street to street and building to building.

Mail carriers work for the government. They get many **benefits**. It's not an easy job though. It's a lot of work to track and deliver all that mail. Mail carriers work almost every day of the year!

office

A job has responsibilities. There are things a person must do for the job.

There are many kinds of jobs in construction. Each job has different responsibilities. **Architects** and **engineers** work together. They plan and build things like homes, offices, schools, and hospitals. Construction workers bring everything together. They read the plans and build the places where we live, study, and work. Construction workers build our communities!

equipment

Construction workers often have a difficult **physical job**. They may have to carry heavy things and work with big pieces of **equipment**. They sometimes work long hours to finish buildings on time. This means they have to work outside when it's cold or raining. Do construction workers stop when the weather is bad? No, they don't. They know their work is important!

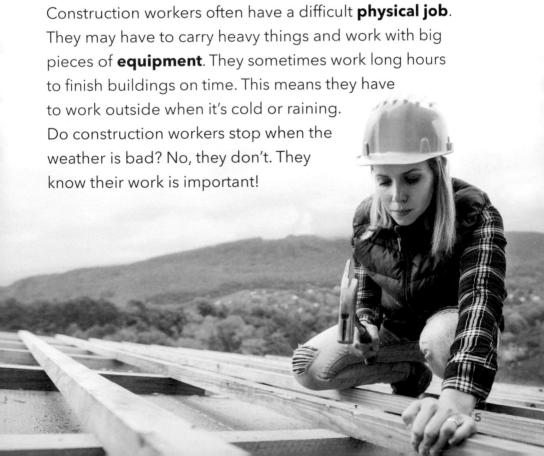

Firefighters work at fire stations. They fight fires in homes and other places. They keep people safe. Firefighters have a dangerous job. Fires can grow large quickly and change at any time!

It's not easy to be a firefighter. Firefighters need a lot of special **skills**. They must be able to use special tools, like ladders and safety equipment. They get special **training** to learn how to fight fires and use their equipment safely.

firefighter training

fire station

FIRE DEPARTMENT

uniform

Firefighters have a physical job, too. They have to be strong and fast because they work in difficult **conditions**. Sometimes they carry people from burning buildings. Other times they have to carry heavy equipment.

Fire stations are open day and night because fires can happen at any time. This means firefighters work long **shifts**. They live and work together as a team. They wear special uniforms to show they're part of this team. The uniforms help protect them on the job as well.

traffic

Police officers wear uniforms, too. Look at this police officer. She's helping direct the traffic. She's keeping the cars and trucks moving on the road. She tells them when to stop and when to go. She also helps people cross the road safely. This is one example of how police officers keep people in cars, homes, and towns safe.

police officers

Police officers get special training, too. They learn how to be safe at work and how to use special equipment.

Sometimes police officers work in a police station. Sometimes they go around towns and cities to check for trouble. Police officers often work in teams, but sometimes they work alone. Every day is different for police officers. They never know what will happen next!

Cashiers work in stores and help customers. They tell customers the prices of things. They also take customers' money and give them change.

There are some disadvantages to being a cashier. They often have to work when other people have free time and go shopping. They often work evenings and weekends. Many cashiers work on holidays, too.

price

cashier

customer

There are advantages to being a cashier as well. They have very useful jobs. It's usually easy for them to find work because so many stores need cashiers. Some small stores may have one or two cashiers, but bigger stores may need hundreds. Another advantage is that stores sometimes give their cashiers discounts. They may even give **employees** things for free!

patient

doctor

medicine

Doctors and nurses usually work in hospitals. They help people who are sick or injured. Some doctors have their own offices where **patients** can come if they don't feel well.

Other doctors work in **laboratories**. They **do research**. They find new ways to help patients and make new medicines.

laboratory

It's not easy to become a doctor or nurse. They must study for many years. They go to special schools to learn all about the body. They also learn how to treat injuries. They learn how to make people feel better. In fact, good doctors and nurses never really stop studying. There are always new illnesses and new medicines to learn about.

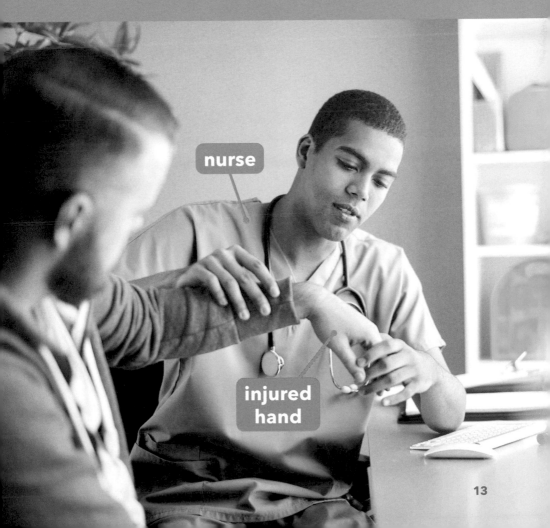

restaurant

take an order

clean the table

server

Servers work in restaurants and cafés. They take orders and bring customers food and drinks. When the customers are finished, servers often clear the tables. They help keep the restaurant clean.

A big advantage for servers can be **tips**. Customers sometimes give them extra money for good service. Restaurants also sometimes give servers free food after their shifts. However, most servers must work very hard. They stand for hours, and they walk a lot, too. They often have sore feet after a shift!

Mail carriers bring us packages and letters. Construction workers build the places where we live and work. Firefighters and police officers keep us, our communities, and our cities safe. Doctors and nurses keep us healthy. Servers and cashiers help us when we shop and eat out.

There are many different jobs to choose from. Each one has advantages and disadvantages. It's up to you to decide: Which job is right for you?

advantage something that gives you a better chance to win or succeed

disadvantage something that works against your chances of winning or succeeding

benefit something helpful and useful

architect a person who makes and draws plans for buildings, bridges, and other construction projects for a job

engineer a person who plans buildings, bridges, and other building projects based on scientific rules and needs

physical job a job that has to do with using the body, such as lifting heavy things

equipment special tools that are used to do certain tasks

skill a special thing that you can do, usually well

training special lessons that are given to help people do a job or task

conditions what a place is like in general; what it looks like, feels like, etc.

shift the period of time that you must work or do a job

employee a person paid to do work for someone else

patient a person who is hurt or sick and under the care of a doctor or in the hospital

laboratory a place where scientists do tests or studies to learn more about something

do research to study something a lot to learn more about it and understand it better

tip money people give for a good or service that is not the cost of the service; extra money given as thanks for a service